Movie Studio Island Adventure

LEVEL 4

Written by: Hawys Morgan
Series Editor: Melanie Williams

Pearson Education Limited
Edinburgh Gate, Harlow,
Essex CM20 2JE, England
and Associated Companies throughout the world.

ISBN: 978-1-4479-7138-2

This edition first published by Pearson Education Ltd 2014

9 10

Set in 17/21pt OT Fiendstar
Printed in Great Britain by Ashford Colour Press Ltd.
SWTC/02

Illustrations: Martyn Cain

For a complete list of the titles available in the Pearson English Kids Readers series, please go to
www.pearsonenglishkidsreaders.com. Alternatively, write to your local Pearson Education office or to
Pearson English Readers Marketing Department, Pearson Education, Edinburgh Gate, Harlow, Essex CM20 2JE, England.

Max and Clara are best friends. Every Saturday after breakfast, they go to the beach on Movie Studio Island. Today, it is a beautiful, sunny day.

"Let's go swimming," says Max.

"Good idea!" says Clara. "Do you have some towels?"

"Yes, I do. My mom gave us some tuna sandwiches, fruit, and juice, too," answers Max.

Max and Clara jump up on a big rock above the ocean. They look down at the beach, where they can see a big ship on the water. "How exciting! Can you see the pirate ship?" asks Max. Before Clara can answer, Max runs quickly down the sandy road to the beach.

They arrive at the beach and stop suddenly, because they are very surprised by what they see. There is a big, old castle on the beach. Clara looks behind it, where she can see a volcano in the thick jungle. How strange! There was *not* a castle *or* a volcano at the beach last week. Where did they come from?

Then, Clara sees a man on the beach who is really worried. "Excuse me. Why is there a ship, a castle, and a volcano at the beach today?" asks Clara.

"I'm Zack. This is my movie set. I'm making a movie about pirates, but I have a big problem," he answers them unhappily. "I can't find the pirate captain's costume."

Captain Crab, the pirate captain, arrives. He and Zack are worried, because they cannot make the movie without the costume. "Can we help you find it?" ask the children.

"Yes, please! Here's a map of the movie set," says Zack.

"And here's the telescope that I use in the movie. Be careful with it!" says Captain Crab.

Zack describes the costume, which Max draws carefully. The mustache is long and black, but the beard is curly and gray. The big, black hat has a red crab on it. There is only one boot, which is brown, silver, and shiny.

"This is the worst day of my life!" cries Captain Crab. "You must find my poor, lovely costume!"

Because the movie set is very big, Max and Clara look at the map carefully before they start. The volcano is in the jungle, which is behind the castle. The castle is on the beach, where they can also see the pirate ship in the ocean.

"Let's look in the castle first," says Clara.
"Okay!" answers Max.

The castle is very big, and very tall. Max looks up at it through the telescope. He can see two brown paws, two arms, two legs, and a tail, but it is shiny, and silver, too. What is it?

Oo Oo!

Look!

It is a monkey. A monkey wearing the pirate's boot! How funny!

Max and Clara climb up the castle to the monkey, but it does not want to give them the pirate's boot.

Yum!

"I know! Let's give him some fruit," says Clara. Max gives the monkey a tasty, yellow banana, which it swaps for the pirate's boot.

"Let's look in the jungle now," says Max.

They walk through the thick jungle between beautiful trees, plants, and flowers. Clara looks through the telescope, and in the highest tree, she sees colorful wings and feathers, but it is big, black, and red, too. What is it?

Squawk!

Look!

It is a parrot. A parrot wearing the pirate's hat! How funny!

Max and Clara sing prettily to the parrot, but it does not want to give them the pirate's hat.

Yum!

"I know! Let's give him some fruit," says Max. Clara gives the parrot a big, juicy orange, which it swaps for the pirate's hat.

"Let's look in the ship now," says Clara.

They swim to the pirate ship, where Max looks through the telescope at the floor of the ship. He can see a brown tail, and small feet, which are moving quickly, but it is gray and curly, too. What is it?

Look!

Squeak!

It is a mouse! A mouse wearing the pirate's beard! How funny!

Max and Clara run here and there after the little, brown mouse, but it is quicker than they are. It does not want to give them the pirate's beard.

Yum!

"I know! Let's give it some fruit!" says Clara. Max gives the mouse a shiny, red apple, which it swaps for the pirate's beard.

But where is the mustache? Clara looks through the telescope at the ocean, where she sees a gray, shiny animal in the water. It is beautiful, and it swims quickly through the water, but it is long and black, too. What is it?

It is a dolphin. A dolphin wearing the pirate's mustache! How funny!

They jump into the water and swim after the dolphin, but it is quicker than they are. It does not want to give them the mustache.

Yum!

"Let's give it some fruit!" says Max.
"Dolphins don't like fruit! Let's give it the tuna sandwiches," laughs Clara. Clara gives the dolphin the sandwiches, which it swaps for the pirate's mustache.

Zack and Captain Crab arrive on the ship, where the children give the boot, the hat, the beard, the mustache, and the telescope back to Captain Crab. He gets dressed in his costume and looks very handsome. At last, they are happy.

"Thank you for your help. You are the best! Now we can make the movie," says Zack.

Before they start to make the movie, Max and Clara ask one last question: "Can we be in the movie? Please?"

"Hmm, I don't know. Can you run, swim, climb, and sing?" asks Zack.

"Yes, we can! We did all those things today," they answer.

"Then yes, you can be pirates in the movie, too," laughs Zack.

Yo ho ho!

Max and Clara get dressed in pirate costumes, which are wonderful. But the animals are really sad, because they want to be in the movie, too.

"Perhaps the animals can be in the movie?" asks Clara.

"Great idea! They are a lot better than these animals made of wood!" answers Zack. "Welcome, all!"

It is twelve o'clock on the movie set. Clara's stomach is a little noisy, and Max's stomach is noisier than Clara's. They are really hungry, because they last ate at breakfast time, which was hours ago! Max looks in his bag, but oh, no! They do not have any fruit or sandwiches left! The animals ate all their lunch.

"Don't worry," says Zack. "You can eat lunch on the movie set, because you're movie stars now. Come on. It's time for lunch!"

Yum!

There are sandwiches, salads, cookies, rice, chicken, cakes, and a lot of fruit! The two hungry little pirates can't wait for their fantastic lunch!

Before You Read

❶ Match the words and pictures.

1 parrot
2 crab
3 pirate captain
4 telescope
5 costume
6 tuna sandwich

❷ Say the places on the map.

After You Read

❶ **Look and match the animals to the pictures. Which things did they wear? Which food did they swap for these things?**

mouse   parrot   monkey   dolphin

❷ **Circle the right answer.**

a The castle is in front of / above the jungle.

b The volcano is behind / in the jungle.

c The ship is next to / above the beach.

d The jungle is under / next to the beach.

e The ship is in / under the ocean.

❸ **Draw a picture of a pirate costume in your exercise book and write about it.**